The Importance of Being Earnest as performed by 3 F**king Queens & A Duck

A play by Steven Dawson

I0449162

Other plays by Steven Dawson published on Lulu.com

Jane Austen's Guide to Pornography

Mr. Braithwaite Has a New Boy

Searching For David

The Adventures of Butt Boy & Tigger

Monstrous Acts

The Importance of Being Earnest as performed by 3 F**king Queens & A Duck

A play by Steven Dawson

Matthew Dorning, Steven Dawson & Lee Threadgold

First Printing: 2015

ISBN 978-1-326-15256-7

Out Cast
PO Box 77
Craigieburn, VIC, AUSTRALIA 3064

www.outcast.org.au

Any application for performance must be made to:

RICK RAFTOS MANAGEMENT
P.O. Box 445, Paddington, NSW, Australia, 2021
raftos@raftos.com.au
Ph:(+612) 9281 9622 Fax:(+612) 9212 7100

Cover Photo by James Penlidis.

The Importance of Being Earnest as performed by 3 F**king Queens & A Duck

A play by Steven Dawson

Characters:

Sebastian	an older actor
Winston –	early 40's
Christian –	mid 20's

First Performance: April 2nd 2013
Mechanics Institute Performing Arts Centre
Melbourne, Australia

Cast:

Sebastian	Steven Dawson
Winston	Lee Threadgold
Christian	Matthew Dorning

Directed by Wayne Pearn
Lighting & Sound by Kieran Hanrahan
Produced by Adrian Corbett & Out Cast Theatre

Setting: A theatre space to resemble a drawing room. The actors in identical Elizabethan breeches, romantic period shirts, tights, ballet slippers and with mop wigs.

The Importance of Being Earnest as performed by 3 F**king Queens & A Duck

A play by Steven Dawson

SCENE ONE

SEBASTIAN AND WINSTON RUN ONSTAGE DRESSED IN HAMMY ACTOR COSTUMES. PUFFED UP BRITCHES, BYRON-ESQUE SHIRTS AND MOP WIGS. WINSTON CARRIES A SMALL WOODEN DUCK UNDER HIS ARM. THEY GLARE AT EACH OTHER AND CIRCLE ROUND EACH OTHER FOR A MOMENT. ALL THEIR STANCES ARE POSED. THEY BOTH SPEAK IN HAMMY VOICES, SEBASTIAN WITH A "W FOR R" SPEECH IMPEDIMENT.

SEBASTIAN
You look good.

WINSTON
And you. Have you been working out?

SEBASTIAN
No need. I have a naturally lithe body.

WINSTON
If you say so. Is it hidden under all that dino-fat?

SEBASTIAN
Well, you have not changed. I can still smell the cheap aftershave. Either that or you've stepped in something.

WINSTON
I like your outfit.

SEBASTIAN
It suits the occasion...

WINSTON
And follows the contours of your form. So are you going to tell me?

SEBASTIAN
In a moment. First there is something I need to address.

WINSTON
Address away.

SEBASTIAN
What's with the duck?

WINSTON
Ah, you noticed. It was a prop used in my last show. You did see it of course.

SEBASTIAN
Alas I was busy that night.

WINSTON
It played 4 weeks.

SEBASTIAN
Alas I was busy that month.

WINSTON
If you say so.

SEBASTIAN
And again I say to you "What's with the duck?"

WINSTON
I have grown attached to it. For some inexplicable reason it comforts me. Whenever my mood becomes low I have but to rub the duck and my mood is altered. It also reminds me of what theatre is all about?

SEBASTIAN
Rub the duck?

WINSTON
It is not just a duck. It is a reminder of why I am in this business of show...business. Even though it is wooden the duck represents life. It is also a symbol of that which is so easy to lose. One's hopes, desires, failures and aspirations.

SEBASTIAN
You get all that from a duck? I heard the show was a pile of pretentious shit. Not you, of course.

WINSTON
Goes without saying.

SEBASTIAN
It is just that one cannot help but think that walking around with a wooden duck reeks of affectation. But again that could be your aftershave.

WINSTON
[IGNORING HIM] As to your call...there was the usual panicked urgency. Not that you are prone to hyperbole.

SEBASTIAN
There is an offer.

WINSTON
I'm listening.

SEBASTIAN
There is a theatre.

WINSTON
Good. No car park Pinter thank you.

SEBASTIAN
There's a theatre available to us for two weeks...gratis.

WINSTON
Gratis?

SEBASTIAN
Free.

WINSTON
I do know *some* Latin. My response was to the hidden obligation implied. Is one to service sexually some benevolent patron or rancid muggins in return?

SEBASTIAN
I doubt it.

WINSTON
I hate the word 'doubt.' It implies vaguery.

SEBASTIAN
You can relax. We have but to stage the event and reap the rewards.

WINSTON
Does one know what the project shall be?

SEBASTIAN
It will be classical.

WINSTON
Good. Had enough of "New Young Thing" theatre with wafer-thin scripts, lovely lighting and 15 minutes scene changes. Do continue.

SEBASTIAN
It will be timeless.

WINSTON
Naturally.

SEBASTIAN
Royalty free.

WINSTON
Goes without saying.

SEBASTIAN
So someone dead obv.

WINSTON
Obv. Small cast?

SEBASTIAN
Uh....

WINSTON
And the play one has in mind?

SEBASTIAN
Mr. Wilde's classic The Importance of Being Earnest.

WINSTON
Good choice.

SEBASTIAN
I thought so.

WINSTON
Big play.

SEBASTIAN
Yes.

WINSTON
Big cast.

SEBASTIAN
Agreed. Cutting would be essential but not if we play most of the characters.

WINSTON
Just the two of us? Lot of work. I don't think I want to work that hard.

SEBASTIAN
You won't hear this often, well not away from the docks anyway, but you need to stretch yourself.

WINSTON
Charming.

SEBASTIAN
And it will not be just the two of us.

WINSTON
No?

SEBASTIAN
No.

WINSTON
Then who else?

CHRISTIAN RUNS ON IN THE SAME COSTUME AS THE OTHERS AND STARES AT THEM.

You have got to be fucking kidding me!

WINSTON CHASES AFTER SEBASTIAN IN A CIRCLE AS CHRISTIAN

STANDS CENTRE.

CHRISTIAN
Winston.

WINSTON
Christian. Sebastian...a word?

HE BAILS SEBASTIAN OVER TO THE SIDE.

Are you, and I'm putting this delicately...off your fucking meds? You asked this little dweeb to be part of the project? He has a dreadful reputation. I heard he once set fire to a set smoking a joint backstage; left a pubic hair on someone's grease stick and no, that's not a euphemism; he's always off his face and worst of all he thinks he's God's gift to the theatre. I also heard he walked out of his last show just days before opening, leaving everyone in the lurch because he didn't feel the need to learn his lines.

SEBASTIAN
I never listen to gossip.

WINSTON
You're a poncy gay actor. Gossip is the only thing that gets your flaps hard.

SEBASTIAN
You call me gay far too often, you know that?

WINSTON
It's hardly a revelation. You're more flaming than a barbeque.

SEBASTIAN
Unlike some my sexuality does not define me.

WINSTON
Try that speech after gargling some rough trade behind a skip.

SEBASTIAN
Marvelous. Can we get back to what we were talking about?

CHRISTIAN
Excuse me. Do I need to be here for this?

SEBASTIAN
[RUSHING TO HIM] Forgive us.

CHRISTIAN
[AVOIDS HIM AND MOVES TO WINSTON] Winston, you look splendid. It's been too long.

WINSTON
Hasn't it just?

CHRISTIAN
I hear you've been in a little show. I'm sorry I didn't get to it. Been a bumper year for me so a tad busy. But well done to you for getting work anyway.

WINSTON
I hear you have been busy as well.

CHRISTIAN
Just the odd bit of telly and a hit play. Did very well.

WINSTON
That must be nice.

CHRISTIAN
It has been.

WINSTON
Oh you're no has-been. You mustn't listen to gossip.

CHRISTIAN
Clever. By the way...nice duck.

WINSTON
Before we go any further I need to ask you something.

CHRISTIAN
Ask away.

WINSTON
Forgive my being blunt but is it true you walked out on your last show mere days before opening?

CHRISTIAN
Ah, the rumour mill *has* been busy. Nothing gets past you.

SEBASTIAN
Not with those hips.

CHRISTIAN
Yes it is true.

WINSTON
I see. Not very professional.

CHRISTIAN
You seem to have an opinion about it already. Had you known the full cir-
cumstances perhaps you would not be so quick to judge. For your info the
situation had become untenable. The director was been making un- welcome
advances on me of a...sexual nature.

WINSTON
You're kidding? And this harassment went on despite his guide dog being in
attendance?

CHRISTIAN
He was grabbing me bits in the rehearsal room, the dirty old bitch, when no-one
was looking.

WINSTON
Bit hypocritical don't you think? I remember a little incident to do with a certain stage manager you had reduced to tears on occasion.

SEBASTIAN
Only when they saw him naked.

CHRISTIAN
Much like success I am ignoring you completely. *[TO WINSTON]* He was a
wimp anyway, that stage manager. I mean really. Who sends flowers to someone
8 hours after a drunken post-show rim-job in the props room? Talk about needy.
In any case I elect to say no more about it. It was my decision to leave the show
and I shall live with the consequences. Now...do you want me for your little
show or what?

SEBASTIAN
I don't know. Winston do we want him for our little show or what?

WINSTON
Is there anyone else?

SEBASTIAN
No.

WINSTON
Do I have a choice?

SEBASTIAN
No.

WINSTON
Then the answer is yes. But if I find a pube on my makeup stick...

CHRISTIAN
What on the where?

SEBASTIAN
Splendid.

CHRISTIAN
So what's the project all about?

SEBASTIAN
The Importance of Being Earnest by Oscar Wilde.

CHRISTIAN
Ooh. Big show.

SEBASTIAN & WINSTON
Yes.

CHRISTIAN
Big cast?

SEBASTIAN & WINSTON
Yes.

CHRISTIAN
Will we make money?

SEBASTIAN & WINSTON
No!

CHRISTIAN
No money you say? But is it a big role?

SEBASTIAN
Roles.

CHRISTIAN
What?

SEBASTIAN
Roles. There will be much doubling required.

CHRISTIAN
Doubling.? How much?

SEBASTIAN
Much!

CHRISTIAN
Much. *[BEAT]* That's a lot. With how many actors again?

SEBASTIAN
Three.

CHRISTIAN
Three actors to perform The Importance of Being Earnest? I am intrigued. Of course it would allow me to run the gamut of my skills.

WINSTON
Yes, both of them.

CHRISTIAN
And the director? Tres important. Who will lead our merry band?

SEBASTIAN
I will be directing of course.

CHRISTIAN
You? Directing *and* acting?

SEBASTIAN
That's right. Problem?

CHRISTIAN
Not at all. I'm just concerned for your workload, that's all. Especially at your advanced age.

SEBASTIAN
Watch it.

CHRISTIAN
Can't have you clutching your chest in the more dramatic moments. You could fall and break something.

SEBASTIAN
Thank you...

CHRISTIAN
Like the set.

SEBASTIAN
Fuck you!

CHRISTIAN
It will all be very challenging. Of course if I *do* do this...

SEBASTIAN & WINSTON
Do-do?

CHRISTIAN
...it will be on one proviso.

WINSTON
One proviso? Who the fuck...?

SEBASTIAN
We are nothing if not accommodating.

CHRISTIAN
Leave your *modus operandi* in the back rooms where it belongs. I am currently seeing someone at the moment. It's all on the hush-hush you understand. He has some little wifey thing on the side apparently so a tad *delicato* but if the position has not already been filled for assistant stage manager I would like him to

take it up, so to speak? He is very reliable and will work for nought. He merely wants to be in my company.

WINSTON
Poor bastard.

CHRISTIAN
Call it a whim.

SEBASTIAN
Have him call me. We shall negotiate the arrangement.

CHRISTIAN
Wonderful.

WINSTON
Wait a minute, wait a minute! Does he have any experience?

CHRISTIAN
Of course. He has worked under me on many occasions.

WINSTON
The price you pay.

CHRISTIAN
Then there is little else to discuss but to all of this I say yes! Yes! A thousand times yes!

WINSTON
Can you get this bitch to dial it down a bit?

CHRISTIAN
Yes. I have suckled on the teet of subsidised theatre for too long. Too safe. My agent will hate me for it but for now it is time to give something back for the sheer art of it. Besides which, there is fuck all else going on.

SEBASTIAN
A noble gesture.

CHRISTIAN
And when are rehearsals to begin?

SEBASTIAN
Tomorrow on the a.m. 10, I should think.

CHRISTIAN
10? Heavens. I shall have to reschedule.

WINSTON
I'm sure the team that waxes your bikini and back hair could do with the day off.

CHRISTIAN
How did you get to be so funny?

WINSTON
Unlike your hairline it's all natural. What's the thread count on that tapestry anyway?

SEBASTIAN
Then it is agreed?

WINSTON
Wait. Sebastian, I *too* have a condition.

SEBASTIAN
And that would be?

WINSTON
I should like to incorporate the duck into the work.

SEBASTIAN
Into The Importance of Being Earnest? I recollect no scenes where wild- life of any description is mentioned.

WINSTON
Never-the-less it is my security blanket. I should not be able to give my best un-less it was placed somewhere about the set or I could even just carry it. As long as it is within eye-line I am well satisfied. We could possibly just add a line.

CHRISTIAN
Add a line to Wilde's hundred year old classic?

SEBASTIAN
I am sure we can...

CHRISTIAN
The purists will be up in arms.

WINSTON
The purists can suck it through an old catheter! It is a 3 hander version of The Importance of Being Earnest. We have already torn the head off it! I want my duck. That is *my* proviso. Call *it* a whim.

CHRISTIAN
[TO SEBASTIAN] Bowing to the talent? Slippery slope, dear, slippery slope. That's all I'm saying. But you know best. See you on the morrow.

CHRISTIAN EXITS. SEBASTIAN STARES AFTER HIM THEN NOTICES WINSTON GLARING AT HIM.

SEBASTIAN
What?

WINSTON
This is a dangerous course, my friend.

SEBASTIAN
He's very talented.

WINSTON
She's hard work. I sense evil.

SEBASTIAN
Nonsense. He will be fine and you will be nice.

WINSTON
I will be gracious at all times.

SEBASTIAN
Good.

PAUSE

WINSTON
Unless the little cunt annoys me.

SEBASTIAN
There you go.

BLACKOUT

SCENE TWO

CHRISTIAN IS RUNNING AROUND THE STAGE TALKING TO HIMSELF, PLAYING BOTH PARTS OF ALGERNON AND JACK, CHANGING POSITIONS AND SPOUTING LINES. SEBASTIAN STANDS TO THE SIDE WATCHING HIM AS WINSTON SITS WITH HIS HEAD IN HIS HANDS OCCASIONALLY LOOKING UP. THERE IS A SMALL TABLE WITH CUCUMBER SANDWICHES ON IT. THE DUCK SITS ON A CHAIR.

CHRISTIAN *[DOING BOTH CHARACTERS QUIETLY TO HIMSELF]*
Jack: When one is in town one amuses oneself. When one is in the country one amuses other people. It is excessively boring.

Algernon: And who are the people you amuse?

Jack: Oh, neighbours, neighbours.

Algernon: Got nice neighbours in your part of Shropshire?

Jack: Perfectly horrid! Never speak to one of them.

Algernon: How immensely you must amuse them! By the way, Shropshire is your county, is it not?

HE REPEATS THE SCENE. THE OTHERS TALK.

WINSTON
It has happened. I have finally lost the will to live. 5 days. 5 days we have been watching this. We haven't even got past the first scene. You need to say something or I will, and I use this term delicately...lose my shit!

SEBASTIAN
It is his process. We must respect the process.

WINSTON
Fuck him and his process right in the ear. You must put your foot down. Give him an inch, he'll multiply it by seven and shove it up his backside! He already minces around like he's left a set of love beads up his guts. Well I say love beads. The size of that trunk it's more like medicine balls on a rope!

SEBASTIAN
He's very good though. Very committed to his craft.

WINSTON
He *should* be committed. Sebastian!

SEBASTIAN
Christian, we must press on.

CHRISTIAN
Oh forgive me. I get so involved I often forget others are at work. I just wanted to be sure but I bow to you, good sir. And where now?

SEBASTIAN
From the start of the scene I should think.

WINSTON
Wait. You forget we still haven't even finalised the roles we are playing.

SEBASTIAN
I thought we had covered most of them.

WINSTON
Most of them yes. One still has to address the elephant in the room.

CHRISTIAN
I think that's unfair. *[TO SEBASTIAN]* I think you've lost quite a bit of weight.

WINSTON
We still haven't settled on Lady B.

SEBASTIAN
Oh I thought that was a given. I think it best if I play Lady Bracknell.

WINSTON
Why?

SEBASTIAN
Clearly I have the age to give it with some credibility.

WINSTON
Clearly you have tickets on yourself.

CHRISTIAN
Hey, why can't I play it?

SEBASTIAN & WINSTON
You?

WINSTON
What a preposterous idea. You're far too young and in any case you're in most of your scenes with her so that rules you out. Jack does most of his talking to Bracknell.

CHRISTIAN
You could do Jack. You're only playing Algy and we've cut out all the Lane, Dr Chausable and Merriman shit.

WINSTON
I'm too old to play Jack.

CHRISTIAN
He's the same age as Algy!

WINSTON
I'm not learning any more fucking lines than I absolutely have to!

CHRISTIAN
I could "age up." You know…put some makeup on.

SEBASTIAN
[LAUGHING] Tooth brush with shoe whitener?

WINSTON
"Tooth brush with shoe whitener." Get fucked.

CHRISTIAN
You can do stuff with lights to make me look older.

SEBASTIAN
Why would we do that when we already have actors old enough to do the bloody role?

CHRISTIAN
I think we…

SEBASTIAN
No, no. As the director I have to put my foot down. I must have the final word on casting.

WINSTON
Well that's that then. So much for democracy.

SEBASTIAN
Whoever told you theatre was a democracy?

CHRISTIAN
I thought theatre was collaborative venture.

SEBASTIAN
Where did you get that pile of piffle? Acting school? We operate in the real world. I'll let you in on a little secret. Most directors only call the process "collaborative" to avoid upsetting whiney designers, stage managers and actors. Nothing to do with theatre. It's all about placating egos. Any director worth his or her salt will tell you it takes all their self- control and NIDA diplomas not to lunge out and smack the annoying little fucks right in the mouth. And as for the actors...instead of constantly giving notes after a so-so performance you'd be better pressed to just take the offending miscreant out to the nearest laneway, drum the stage directions into them with a sack of horse shit and give them a righteous kick in the dick to close the deal!

WINSTON
I'm glad we know where we stand.

SEBASTIAN
Not that I think that of you. You're both marvelous and I utterly treasure our moments together.

CHRISTIAN
Thank you.

WINSTON
Yes, thanks.

SEBASTIAN
Now shall we get back to what we were talking about?

WINSTON
You playing Lady Bracknell?

SEBASTIAN
Well, as long as we're all agreed. Now how about we move on?

CHRISTIAN
Sebastian, I think we are approaching this all wrong.

WINSTON
Sweet Jesus.

SEBASTIAN
Really?

CHRISTIAN
Yes. I thought it might be interesting if we tried some different way of interpreting the text. I've been doing a few classes at Fourteenth Street...

SEBASTIAN
Oh get fucked! That pile of bilious bullshit. Name me one actor who came out of that joint and actually did something worthwhile. Idiot actors with too much money paying other third rate actors pretending to be teachers. Now *that's* great acting. I had one dickhead drop out of a play because he didn't want to miss a few classes. Call me old fashioned but maybe actually "doing a show" would be the best training that dickhead would get!

WINSTON
Well said, darling. That should win you friends.

SEBASTIAN
You were saying?

CHRISTIAN
Are you sure the style we are performing it in is best? Maybe we should approach it from a different direction. It doesn't have to be so naturalistic. This walking around like we've got a stick up our arse....

WINSTON
Medicine ball.

CHRISTIAN
What?

WINSTON
Nothing.

CHRISTIAN
It's all been done before.

SEBASTIAN
And worked, I might add. Let's not fuck with the wheel. Now can we please get back to work? Jack and Gwendolen's scene thank you.

CHRISTIAN
Which scene is that?

SEBASTIAN
The one where they talk to each other. The sodding proposal.

CHRISTIAN
Gotcha.

SEBASTIAN
Christian, you're Jack. Winston...you're Gwendolen. From the "married Mr. Worthing" line. Go.

CHRISTIAN *[AS JACK]*
Gwendolen, I must get christened at once - I mean we must get married at once. There is no time to be lost.

WINSTON *[AS GWENDOLEN]*
Married, Mr. Worthing?

CHRISTIAN *[AS JACK]*
Well... surely. You know that I love you, and you led me to believe, Miss Fairfax, that you were not absolutely indifferent to me.

DURING THE SCENE SEBASTIAN MOVES AROUND, MOUTHING THE WORDS AND HELPING HIMSELF TO THE CUCUMBER SANDWICHES.

WINSTON *[AS GWENDOLEN]*
I adore you. But you haven't proposed to me yet. Nothing has been said at all about marriage. The subject has not even been touched on.

CHRISTIAN *[AS JACK]*
Well... may I propose to you now?

WINSTON *[AS GWENDOLEN]*
I think it would be an admirable opportunity. And to spare you any possible dis-

appointment, Mr. Worthing, I think it only fair to tell you quite frankly before-hand that I am fully determined to accept you.

CHRISTIAN *[AS JACK]*
Gwendolen!

WINSTON *[AS GWENDOLEN]*
Yes, Mr. Worthing, what have you got to say to me?

CHRISTIAN *[AS JACK]*
You know what I have got to say to you.

WINSTON *[AS GWENDOLEN]*
Yes, but you don't say it.

CHRISTIAN *[AS JACK]*
Gwendolen, will you marry me?

WINSTON *[AS GWENDOLEN]*
Of course I will, darling. How long you have been about it! I am afraid you have had very little experience in how to propose.

CHRISTIAN *[AS JACK]*
My own one, I have never loved anyone in the world but you.

WINSTON *[AS GWENDOLEN]*
Yes, but men often propose for practice. I know my brother Gerald does. All my girl-friends tell me so. What wonderfully blue eyes you have, Ernest!

CHRISTIAN WALKS AWAY FROM THE SCENE, CHECKING HIS MOBILE PHONE.

They are quite, quite, blue. I hope you will always look at me just like that, especially when there are other people present."...I'm sorry. Have we stopped?

CHRISTIAN
I'm sorry Winston...Sebastian. I'm just not feeling it.

WINSTON
Well, we can't have that.

CHRISTIAN
I just think it's all rather boring and stuffy.

SEBASTIAN
Oscar Wilde is *not* boring and stuffy!

WINSTON
Of course he is.

SEBASTIAN
Whose side are you on?

WINSTON
In this case the kid's.

SEBASTIAN
Oh. So *you* think we should do it a little different as well?

WINSTON
Can't hurt. Let's face it, unless you are doing something extraordinary it's just one-liner after one-liner with posh voices sounding like you've got a plummy knob in your gob.

THEY ALL LOOK TO AUDIENCE THEN BACK.

SEBASTIAN
So what would you have us do? Cartwheels with sparklers flying out our arses?

WINSTON
Anything to take the focus away from your face.

SEBASTIAN
What did you have in mind?

CHRISTIAN
Something edgier. Not the lines of course. Just in the playing of it.

WINSTON
Jesus, what do you want? A bit of biffo Berkoff?

SEBASTIAN
Heaven forbid.

LIGHTS CHANGE. THEY DO THE SAME SCENE AGAIN BUT IN A HARD AGRESSIVE STYLE WITH EAST END ACCENTS. THEY TOUCH THEMSELVES THROUGHOUT. SEBASTIAN LOOKS ON, INCREASINGLY HORRIFIED.

CHRISTIAN *[AS JACK]*
Gwendolen, I must get christened at once - I mean we must get married at once. There is no time to be lost.

WINSTON *[AS GWENDOLEN]*
Married, Mr. Worthing?

CHRISTIAN *[AS JACK]*
Well... surely. You know that I love you, and you led me to believe, Miss Fairfax, that you were not absolutely indifferent to me, ya' slag!

WINSTON *[AS GWENDOLEN]*
I adore you. But you haven't proposed to me yet. Nothing has been said at all about marriage. The subject has not even been touched on.

CHRISTIAN *[AS JACK]*
Well... may I propose to you now?

WINSTON *[AS GWENDOLEN]*
I think it would be an admirable opportunity. And to spare you any possible disappointment, Mr. Worthing, I think it only fair to tell you quite frankly beforehand that I am fully determined to accept you.

CHRISTIAN *[AS JACK]*
Gwendolen!

WINSTON *[AS GWENDOLEN]*
Yes, Mr. Worthing, what have you got to say to me?

CHRISTIAN *[AS JACK]*
You know what I have got to say to you.

WINSTON *[AS GWENDOLEN]*
Yes, but you don't say it.

CHRISTIAN *[AS JACK]*
Gwendolen, will you marry me?

WINSTON *[AS GWENDOLEN]*
Of course I will, darling. *[THEY START DRY HUMPING]* How long you have been about it! I am afraid you have had very little experience in how to propose.

CHRISTIAN *[AS JACK]*
My own one, I have never loved anyone in the world but you.

WINSTON *[AS GWENDOLEN]*
Yes, but men often propose for practice. I know my brother Gerald does.

BOTH
Cunt!

WINSTON *[AS GWENDOLEN]*
All my girl-friends tell me so.

BOTH
Slags!

SEBASTIAN
Enough!

WINSTON
Thank fuck. Only acting students do Berkoff these days anyway. Along with infinite all-male versions of The Maids. Men in dresses. How innovative.

CHRISTIAN
Just think it needs something else. Could be interesting.

WINSTON
I've always liked the visuals of Kabuki. *[HE PRONOUNCES IT KAR-BOO-KYE]*

SEBASTIAN & CHRISTIAN
Kabuki?

WINSTON
Do you think we could incorporate that kind of thing?

SEBASTIAN
I really don't think....

WINSTON
Come on. This will be fun.

DRAMATIC LIGHTING. LOUD GONG AND DRUMS AS THEY PLAY OUT
THE SCENE AGAIN WITH SNARLS AND GROWLS AND VERY SLOW.
SEBASTIAN LOOKS CONFUSED.

CHRISTIAN *[AS JACK]*
Gwendolen, I must get christened at once - I mean we must get married at once.
There is no time to be lost.

WINSTON *[AS GWENDOLEN]*
Married, Mr. Worthing?

CHRISTIAN *[AS JACK]*
[ASTOUNDED] Well... surely. You know that I love you, and you led me to
believe, Miss Fairfax, that you were not absolutely indifferent to me, ya' slag!

WINSTON *[AS GWENDOLEN]*
I adore you. But you haven't proposed to me yet. Nothing has been said at all
about marriage. The subject has not even been touched on.

CHRISTIAN *[AS JACK]*
Well... may I propose to you now?

WINSTON *[AS GWENDOLEN]*
I think it would be an admirable opportunity. And to spare you any possible disappointment, Mr. Worthing, I think it only fair to tell you quite frankly before-
hand that I am fully determined to accept you.

SEBASTIAN CUTS THEM OFF AGAIN.

SEBASTIAN
Hi-ya-ku! Hi-ya-ku! Ba-ka-des! *[Hurry! Hurry! Idiot!]*

THEY STOP. CHRISTIAN WINCES.

CHRISTIAN
I think I pulled something.

SEBASTIAN
Well, that was just plain ridic...

WINSTON
Go for more natural. Chekhov if you please.

HE WHIPS THE SMALL TABLE CLOTH FROM UNDER THE SANDWICHES AND USES IT AS A SHAWL. ALL THREE STAND CLOSE TOGETHER LOOKING OFF INTO THE DISTANCE AND START PLAYNG THE SCENE AGAIN. SOFT BABALAIKA MUSIC. ALL 3 ACTORS ARE ALMOST SOBBING.

CHRISTIAN *[AS JACK]*
Gwendolen, I must get christened at once - I mean we must get married at once. There is no time to be lost.

WINSTON *[AS GWENDOLEN]*
Married, Mr. Worthing?

CHRISTIAN *[AS JACK]*
Well... surely. You know that I love you, and you led me to believe, Miss Fairfax, that you were not absolutely indifferent to me, ya' slag!

WINSTON *[AS GWENDOLEN]*
I adore you. But you haven't proposed to me yet. Nothing has been said at all about marriage. The subject has not even been touched on.

CHRISTIAN *[AS JACK]*
Well... may I propose to you now?

WINSTON *[AS GWENDOLEN]*
I think it would be an admirable opportunity. And to spare you any possible disappointment, Mr. Worthing, I think it only fair to tell you quite frankly beforehand that I am fully determined to accept you.

THEY STEP BACK THEN BREAK INTO A VAUDEVILLE RENDITION OF "UNDERNEATH THE ARCHES." IN THE MIDDLE THE SOUND OF A VIBRATING PHONE CAN BE HEARD. THEY STOP AND LOOK AT CHRISTIAN AS HE TAKES A MOBILE OUT OF HIS PANTS AND CHECKS MESSAGES. THE OTHERS GLARE AT HIM, AT EACH OTHER THEN BACK AT HIM. THEIR EXPRESSIONS GOES OVERBOARD.

WINSTON
If you don't put that phone down I am going to shove it so far up your arse you'll be tweeting with your tongue!

CHRISTIAN
Sorry, just promo-ing the play. A few casting agents want to come and see. *[SEBASTIAN AND WINSTON LOOK AT EACH OTHER]* Silly really. They could just as easily get my show-reel from my agent. The twitter-verse is very excited about it.

WINSTON AND SEBASTIAN SIDLE UP TO HIM

WINSTON
Casting agents you say?

CHRISTIAN
I know. Such a bore. Shall we continue?

WINSTON
Have we decided on a style?

CHRISTIAN
Oh now that I think of it, it's all too taxing. Perhaps we should leave it as is. As you say, "mustn't fuck with the wheel."

SEBASTIAN
I think it best.

WINSTON
Oops. Excuse me for a moment. I have to make a dash to the little boys room.

SEBASTIAN
Will you be long?

WINSTON
Need to push a cow in the Ganges, I'm afraid.

SEBASTIAN
Vivid.

WINSTON RUSHES OUT. SEBASTIAN SITS DOWN WHILE CHRISTIAN HELPS HIMSELF TO THE SANDWICHES.

Well.

CHRISTIAN
Yes. Well.

SEBASTIAN
So how are you going then?

CHRISTIAN
Good, good. You?

SEBASTIAN
Fine, fine. By the way, saw your last show. You were very good, very brave.

CHRISTIAN
Thanks.

SEBASTIAN
Especially the nude scene. It was all out there, wasn't it?

CHRISTIAN
Meh. Nudes scenes are just another thing you have to do sometimes. As long as it's integral to the plot and part of the story.

SEBASTIAN
Who would've thought the Cherry Orchard *needed* a nude scene? But you showed them, didn't you? *[UNDER HIS BREATH]* Both of them. *[PAUSE]* So...you're settling in well by the looks of it. Winston seems to have grown accustomed to your face.

CHRISTIAN
When he's not wanting to tear it off, you mean.

SEBASTIAN
Oh, take no notice. Underneath that school ma'am exterior there's a...

CHRISTIAN
Bitter fuck?

SEBASTIAN
I was going to say "gentle giant" but that works as well.

THEY LAUGH AWKWARDLY.

CHRISTIAN
You've worked together a lot haven't you?

SEBASTIAN
Winston and myself? Yes. Many years. Many, *many* years. He's been around forever. They say you can see the candles on his birthday cake from space.

CHRISTIAN
He's very good looking.

SEBASTIAN
You know, I've never noticed.

CHRISTIAN
For an older man, that is. Not that I'm really into older men as a rule.

SEBASTIAN
Aren't you? Well, bully for you.

CHRISTIAN
Not that I wouldn't contemplate *being* with an older man. Just not yet. Maybe when I'm really old myself. In my forties or something.

SEBASTIAN
Aren't you a treasure?

CHRISTIAN
Thanks.

SEBASTIAN
*[UNDER HIS BRREATH] W*ell, I'd like to bury you.

CHRISTIAN
What?

SEBASTIAN
Nothing.

CHRISTIAN
So do you think we can get it together in time? The show, I mean.

SEBASTIAN
I have faith. You know what they say…"Just keep swimming, just keep swimming." Though sometimes it's like doing backstroke through the primary tank at a treatment farm.

WINSTON ENTERS.

Speaking of which.

WINSTON
Well, *that* was all sound and no fury. Don't worry. They're all dead. Never let 'em go full term. That's my motto.

SEBASTIAN
Classy as well.

WINSTON
Oh, by the way. There's some stranger wandering around in the foyer.

CHRISTIAN
Short? Freckly?

WINSTON
Freckly? Looks like she's been slapped in the face with fishnets full of shit!

CHRISTIAN
That'll be my friend. You know...the one I was telling you about?

WINSTON
Really?

CHRISTIAN
Uh-huh.

WINSTON
And he's bisexual right?

CHRISTIAN
Yes.

WINSTON
Okay, if you say so.

WINSTON WALKS AWAY ROLLING HIS EYES. HE LEANS IN TO SEBASTIAN.

Looks like she's just been pushed off a parade float, .lips first. Definitely a member of the orchestra.

SEBASTIAN
What?

WINSTON
Player of the pink oboe? *[TO CHRISTIAN]* I told him you'll be out in an hour. *[TO SEBASTIAN]* That's okay, isn't it?

SEBASTIAN
Of course.

CHRISTIAN
Where to now, El Capitano?

SEBASTIAN
Oh, ah...

WINSTON
Ooh, I have an idea. Perhaps we should do the Bracknell scene?

SEBASTIAN
Oh, I'm not fully comfortable with the lines yet.

WINSTON
Oh, nonsense. We can prompt you. Not that you'll need it. After all, as a director you should know every beat of this beast. You know every beat everywhere else.

SEBASTIAN
Very well. *[AS LADY BRACKNELL] Take a seat, Mr. Worthing.*

CHRISTIAN
Oh shit. That bit. *[AS JACK]* Thank you, Lady Bracknell, I prefer standing.

SEBASTIAN *[AS LADY BRACKNELL]*
I feel bound to tell you that you are not down on my list of eligible young men. However, I am quite ready to enter your name, should your answers be what a really affectionate mother requires. Do you smoke?

CHRISTIAN *[AS JACK]*
Well, yes, I must admit I smoke.

SEBASTIAN *[AS LADY BRACKNELL]*
I am glad to hear it. A man should always have an occupation of some kind. How old are you?

CHRISTIAN *[AS JACK]*
Twenty-nine.

SEBASTIAN *[AS LADY BRACKNELL]*
A very good age to be married at. I have always been of opinion that a man who desires to get married should know either everything or nothing. Which do you know?

CHRISTIAN *[AS JACK]*
I know nothing, Lady Bracknell.

SEBASTIAN *[AS LADY BRACKNELL]*
I am pleased to hear it. What is your income?

CHRISTIAN *[AS JACK]*
Between seven and eight thousand a year.

SEBASTIAN *[AS LADY BRACKNELL]*
In land, or in investments?

CHRISTIAN *[AS JACK]*
In investments, chiefly.

SEBASTIAN *[AS LADY BRACKNELL]*
That is satisfactory. What between the duties expected of one during one's life-time, and the duties exacted from one after ones death, land has ceased to be either a profit or a pleasure.

CHRISTIAN *[AS JACK]*
I have a country house with some land, of course, attached to it, about fifteen hundred acres, I believe; but I don't depend on that for my real income…

SEBASTIAN *[AS LADY BRACKNELL]*
A country house! You have a town house, I hope? A girl with a simple, un-spoiled nature, like Gwendolen, could hardly be expected to reside in the country.

CHRISTIAN *[AS JACK]*
Well, I own a house in Belgrave Square, but it is let by the year to Lady Blox-ham. Of course, I can get it back whenever I like, at six months no- tice.

SEBASTIAN *[AS LADY BRACKNELL*
Lady Bloxham? I don't know her.

CHRISTIAN *[AS JACK]*
Oh, she goes about very little. She is a lady considerably advanced in years.

SEBASTIAN *[AS LADY BRACKNELL]*
Ah, nowadays that is no guarantee of respectability of character. What are your politics?

CHRISTIAN *[AS JACK]*
Well, I am afraid I really have none. I am a Liberal Unionist.

SEBASTIAN *[AS LADY BRACKNELL]*
Oh, they count as Tories. They dine with us. Or come in the evening, at any rate. Now to minor matters. Are your parents living?

CHRISTIAN *[AS JACK]*
I have lost both my parents.

SEBASTIAN *[AS LADY BRACKNELL]*
To lose one parent, Mr. Worthing, may be regarded as a misfortune; to lose both looks like carelessness. Who was your father?

CHRISTIAN *[AS JACK]*
I am afraid I really don't know. The fact is, Lady Bracknell, I said I had lost my parents. It would be nearer the truth to say that my parents seem to have lost me... I don't actually know who I am by birth. I was... well, I was found.

SEBASTIAN *[AS LADY BRACKNELL]*
Found!

CHRISTIAN *[AS JACK]*
The late Mr. Thomas Cardew, an old gentleman of a very charitable and kindly disposition, found me, and gave me the name of Worthing, be- cause he hap- pened to have a first-class ticket for Worthing in his pocket at the time. Worthing is a place in Sussex. It is a seaside resort.

SEBASTIAN *[AS LADY BRACKNELL]*
Where did the charitable gentleman who had a first-class ticket for this seaside resort find you?

CHRISTIAN *[AS JACK]*
In a hand-bag.

SEBASTIAN *[AS LADY BRACKNELL]*
[OVER THE TOP] A handbag?

CHRISTIAN *[AS JACK]*
Yes, Lady Bracknell. I was in a handbag - a somewhat large, black leather hand-bag, with handles to it. An ordinary hand-bag in fact.

SEBASTIAN *[AS LADY BRACKNELL]*
In what locality did this Mr. James, or Thomas, Cardew come across this ordinary hand-bag?

CHRISTIAN *[AS JACK]*
In the cloak-room at Victoria Station. It was given to him in mistake for his own. The Brighton line I believe.

SEBASTIAN *[AS LADY BRACKNELL]*
The line is immaterial. Mr. Worthing, I confess I feel somewhat bewildered by what you have just told me...

WINSTON
If I might cut in...

SEBASTIAN
What? Oh please do. I wasn't doing anything important.

WINSTON
Clearly. That line.

SEBASTIAN
Line? Which line? The Brighton line?

WINSTON
You know very well the line I am talking about. The handbag line.

SEBASTIAN
What about it?

WINSTON
Is that really the way you're going to do it?

SEBASTIAN
Of course. Why?

WINSTON
Well it's just that it is one of the most famous lines on the English stage. I just wonder whether you are giving it the weight it warrants.

SEBASTIAN
Short of pulling a set of butcher's scales out of my arse I think I am giving it the precise weight it deserves. You think you could deliver it better?

WINSTON
I think Dominos could deliver it better! I think it needs a little more oomph. Perhaps the whole voice is wrong. Who are you supposed to be anyway?

SEBASTIAN
What do you mean who am I supposed to be?

CHRISTIAN
Anyway...

SEBASTIAN
I am no one. I am Lady Bracknell.

WINSTON
She's an elderly matriarch. You've got her as a bag lady who just had her shopping trolley nicked. You need to make her more base-y.

SEBASTIAN
What? Like Count Basie?

WINSTON
No. A bit more timbre. *[OVER THE TOP]* *["A handbag?"* That sort of thing. Just a suggestion.

CHRISTIAN
Maybe a Scottish accent? *"A handbag?"* See?

WINSTON
That is the worst Scottish accent I have ever heard. Do it more like this.

WINSTON AND CHRISTIAN START DOING THE WORD HANDBAG WITH VARYING ACCENTS.AFTER A WHILE...

SEBASTIAN
Oh, for fuck's sake! I think I know a *little* about acting. I have been doing it

for...oh, let's see, thirty five fucking years! *[POINTING AT CHRISTIAN]* I've got teeth marks on my dick older than you so how about the both of you let me be the best judge on my performance?

WINSTON
I'm not having a go at you. I'm just saying.

SEBASTIAN
Then say it a little quieter! It's a work in progress!

WINSTON
As long as that's what it is.

SEBASTIAN
What do you mean by....

THE SOUND OF A MOBILE PHONE. THEY GLARE AT CHRISTIAN. HE LOOKS BEWILDERED. SEBASTIAN THEN REALISES IT IS HIS MOBILE. HE IS EMBARRASSED. HE ANSWERS IT.

Yes? Oh. *[TO OTHERS]* Excuse me a moment won't you? Business to take care of. Why don't you run the Cecily and Gwendolen scene, okay? Hurry up Gwendolen or I'll kick you in the tit!

HE EXITS AS THE OTHERS LOOK AT EACH OTHER.

WINSTON
Right...

THEY BOTH SIT ON THE EDGE OF THE SAME CHAIR LOOKING AWAY FROM EACH OTHER. AS THE SCENE PROGRESSES IT TAKES ON DECIDEDLY LESBIAN OVERTONES.

WINSTON *[AS GWENDOLEN]*
Your guardian?

CHRISTIAN *[AS CECILY]*
Yes, I am Mr. Worthing's ward.

WINSTON *[AS GWENDOLEN]*
Oh! It is strange he never mentioned to me that he had a ward. How secretive of him! if I may speak candidly…

CHRISTIAN *[AS CECILY]*
Pray do! I think that whenever one has anything unpleasant to say, one should always be quite candid.

WINSTON *[AS GWENDOLEN]*
Well, to speak with perfect candour, Cecily, I wish that you were fully forty-two, and more than usually plain for your age. Ernest has a strong upright nature. But even men of the noblest possible moral character are extremely susceptible to the influence of the physical charms of others.

CHRISTIAN *[AS CECILY]*
I beg your pardon, Gwendolen, did you say Ernest?

WINSTON *[AS GWENDOLEN]*
Yes.

CHRISTIAN *[AS CECILY]*
Oh, but it is not Mr. Ernest Worthing who is my guardian. It is his brother. His elder brother.

WINSTON *[AS GWENDOLEN]*
Ernest never mentioned to me that he had a brother.

CHRISTIAN *[AS CECILY]*
I am sorry to say they have not been on good terms for a long time.

WINSTON *[AS GWENDOLEN]*
Ah! that accounts for it. And now that I think of it I have never heard any man mention his brother. The subject seems distasteful to most men. Cecily, you have lifted a load from my mind. I was growing almost anxious. It would have been terrible if any cloud had come across a friendship like ours, would it not? Of course you are quite, quite sure that it is not Mr. Ernest Worthing who is your guardian?

CHRISTIAN *[AS CECILY]*
Quite sure. In fact, I am going to be his.

WINSTON *[AS GWENDOLEN]*
I beg your pardon?

CHRISTIAN LUNGES FORWARD AND KISSES WINSTON JUST AS SEBASTIAN WALKS BACK IN STILL ON HIS MOBILE. HE DOES A QUICK U- TURN AND WALKS OUT.

WINSTON
Where the fuck did that come from?

CHRISTIAN
I'm sorry. I'm sorry.

WINSTON
What are you thinking?

CHRISTIAN
I'm just a little stressed, is all. I've been under a bit of pressure lately what with the show and now I think Freddy is leaving me.

WINSTON
Freddy? Who the fuck is Freddy?

CHRISTIAN
Our assistant stage manager. The one I've been seeing.

WINSTON
The one waiting outside? The one with the "wife?"

CHRISTIAN
Uh-huh.

WINSTON
So, because he's dumping you, that's the reason you slap your chops all over your fellow actor?

CHRISTIAN
I don't think of you as an actor.

WINSTON
Thank you.

CHRISTIAN
We've already done one other show together. I consider you more like my friend.

WINSTON
Keep that to yourself. I have a reputation to maintain.

CHRISTIAN
I just don't have many people to talk to about this kind of thing. Too many burnt bridges I'm afraid.

WINSTON
Well just you keep sleeping with married men. That should earn you some serious stripes for a start.

CHRISTIAN
Sorry about the kissing. My emotions are all over the shop. Don't know whether I'm Arthur or Martha.

WINSTON
Oh that's too easy. Stop laying them out like that. And about the kissing? Think nothing of it. I certainly do. So...this Freddy person who is about to dump your arse? If you think he's going to leave why stay?

CHRISTIAN
Because like every second straight guy I meet these days, 2 drinks into them and they suck like a potty calf and take it like a chook!

WINSTON ALMOST CHOKES ON HIS DRINK.

And I'm over sleeping with *gay* men these days anyway. It's all too easy.

WINSTON
That's not the only thing that's easy.

CHRISTIAN
I wish I was more like you. You know that. You don't let anything get in.

WINSTON
Oh, the hymen rotted out years ago. It's all I can do to stop my lungs dropping out and dragging on the tufted shag.

CHRISTIAN
I do admire you, you know. From the very first time I saw you on stage I admired you. Of course I was just a child of 13 or 14.

WINSTON
Were you just? Well, thanks. I will of course continue to treat you like shit but thanks.

SEBASTIAN ENTERS

SEBASTIAN
Are you two okay?

CHRISTIAN
Fine, fine.

WINSTON
Couldn't be better.

SEBASTIAN
We have a problem.

WINSTON
Problem? Of course we have a problem. One bullet should fix it.

SEBASTIAN
Management has asked if we can drop the show down to 90 minutes. All of a sudden they've had some interest in the venue from paying parties. We need to cut more.

WINSTON
From a 2 hour play?

SEBASTIAN
We shall just have to be ruthless. Cut to the bare bones.

WINSTON
Why not.

SEBASTIAN
I shall have to sleep on it.

WINSTON
Good.

CHRISTIAN
That's it for today then?

SEBASTIAN
I suppose.

CHRISTIAN
So it's safe for me to go?

SEBASTIAN
Get out or I'll kill you.

CHRISTIAN
Great.

CHRISTIAN RUNS OFF.

WINSTON
And that's me off home then. I think I shall recline on my Jason, pop on some Nigerian porn and quaff a goon bag of Chateau Face.

SEBASTIAN GLARES AT WINSTON.

What? Sir, you look at me like I have a cat turd on me toupee?

SEBASTIAN
I have only one thing to say to you.

WINSTON
That should make a change. What?

SEBASTIAN
How dare you!

WINSTON
Well, that's succinct. Easy on the details dear. I'll get confused.

SEBASTIAN
Taking advantage of that young man. You're old enough to be his father.

WINSTON
That's two things but math was never your strong suit. Whatever you've got going on in that tiny brain is confused.

SEBASTIAN
You kissed him!

WINSTON
Er...he kissed me.

SEBASTIAN
Liar!

WINSTON
I'm not sure I care for your tone or the insinuation.

SEBASTIAN
He has a boyfriend you know.

WINSTON
So? People with boyfriends don't kiss other people?

SEBASTIAN
Not if they have morals.

WINSTON
He's a fucking actor. After their gag reflex morals are the first thing to go! Oh I get it. You've got the hots for him. You've got the hots for him so he's out of bounds? Is that it?

SEBASTIAN
What a load of rubbish!

WINSTON
I've seen the way you've been checking him out. Maybe the lines are get- ting a little blurry. A director fancying his actor. The most predictable thing next to politicians bumming rent boys.

SEBASTIAN
Just a bit of friendly advice. Try and keep your libido in your tights. At least until the show's over and I will say no more about it.

WINSTON
I think it wise.

SEBASTIAN
Otherwise we may come to blows.

WINSTON
Well...Christian and I might. We shall see.

WINSTON MIMES GIVING HEAD. SEBASTIAN STORMS OFF, DISGUSTED.

BLACKOUT.

<u>SCENE THREE</u>

WINSTON IS STANDNG BY THE SIDE OF THE STAGE PEERING THROUGH AN INVISIBLE CURTAIN. CHRISTIAN COMES UP BEHIND HIM AND STARTS GROPING HIM.

WINSTON
Stop it you bloody idiot! Try to be professional. You want Sebastian or Freddy to see?

CHRISTIAN
Freddy can go fuck himself. Where's Sebastian? Some old dude out in the foyer asked me to give him a letter.

WINSTON
Haven't seen him since the half.

CHRISTIAN
What's the crowd like?

WINSTON
Absolutely rank and file. Just a lot of foo-foo burgers and senior citz expecting cock.

CHRISTIAN
Boy, did they get it wrong with this one.

WINSTON
Sebastian does seem to attract a niche market. No sign of any casting agents?

CHRISTIAN
Let's see. *[LOOKS OUT AGAIN]* Lonely overweight women and skinny queens as their plus ones? Nope.

WINSTON
I thought you said the twitter-verse was abuzz?

CHRISTIAN
Hot and cold darling, hot and cold. By the way are you coming over after the show?

WINSTON
After blowing me off last night? I think not.

CHRISTIAN
I had a prior engagement.

WINSTON
If you say so.

CHRISTIAN
Come one. I'll make it up to you.

WINSTON
Obv you're over what's his name. Look, can you at least focus for a minute on
the important things?

CHRISTIAN
I am.

WINSTON
We have a show to do. I'm already shitting myself eight shades of guano and
you're so nonplussed you could blend into the set.

CHRISTIAN
I'm fine. You shouldn't get worked up. It's just a show.

WINSTON
Oh Christ, you've smoked something, haven't you?

CHRISTIAN
I just had a little toke. Calms me.

WINSTON
We are about to go on in 20 minutes and you're off with the pixies?

CHRISTIAN
I am fine. Stop getting so worked up.

WINSTON
So all the rumours were true?

CHRISTIAN
Mustn't believe everything you hear.

WINSTON
You *did* burn down that set backstage.

CHRISTIAN
It was an accident. *[SMIRKING]* Sometimes you *"do what you gotta do"* to get out of a shit show. Besides we're lovers now. We shouldn't have any secrets.

WINSTON
Good God! We are not lovers. I fucked you once. I was drunk, you were easy. Ta-da. That's it. Let's get back to something a little more tangible. There are some people in this business that take their craft very seriously. I don't think I can even contemplate any kind of a relationship with someone who is so reckless with their craft! We have a duty to the theatre!

CHRISTIAN
Hey, hey, hey….hey…hey. It's okay babe. Chill. It will all be fine.

WINSTON
Oh fuck off hippy!

HE KNEES CHRISTIAN IN THE GROIN AND TURNS JUST AS SEBASTIAN ENTERS IN FULL LADY BRACKNELL COSTUME.

What the fuck are you wearing?

SEBASTIAN
Oh this old thing? Had it for hours. Shirley at the MTC wardrobe was very obliging.

WINSTON
Shirley gave you that? She never mentioned…I thought we agreed we weren't having costumes? "Let our acting carry the show" you said.

SEBASTIAN
It's just for Bracknell. I am using it as a device.

WINSTON
A device?

SEBASTIAN
Yes. If one person stands out it makes the others the focus. You never notice the queen bee. You only notice the drones buzzing about. It brings the focus back to

the minor characters on stage.

WINSTON
Minor characters? What kind of bullshit psychology is that? This is not what we agreed.

SEBASTIAN
Nevertheless I am the director and that is my final word. I will dress up and you can wear your lightly coloured gay apparel.

WINSTON
Excuse me a moment. I left something in my car.

WINSTON RUNS OFFSTAGE. CHRISTIAN ROLLS FLAT ON HIS BACK.

SEBASTIAN
Are you alright? Why are you on the ground? You're not ill, are you? Jesus, that's all we need.

CHRISTIAN
No, I'm okay. Just resting me nads.

SEBASTIAN
Well suck it up princess. We have a job to do and this is *"theatre."*

CHRISTIAN
Oh, some old dude gave me this to give you.

HE HANDS SEBASTIAN THE LETTER.

SEBASTIAN
What now? *[READS THE LETTER]*

CHRISTIAN
Sebastian, I was just thinking during the Gwendolen and Cecily scene maybe we could make it a little more lezzo. You know. Fuck with the audience a bit. Maybe even have a kiss. I don't know. You're the director. You decide.

SEBASTIAN
Oh for Christmas panto! Now they need us to drop the show down to 45 minutes. There's a football team coming in for an after-game booze-up and they're paying a lot of money for the venue.

CHRISTIAN
Football players you say? When?

SEBASTIAN
Tonight.

CHRISTIAN
[GETTING UP] Tonight?

SEBASTIAN
What to do, what to do? We shall just have to cut on the fly.

CHRISTIAN
Cut on the fly? Boy this is really freaking me out.

SEBASTIAN
Get a fucking grip! Try to act like a professional for heaven's sakes!
Where the hell is Winston?

HE STARTS TO WALK OFF AND STOPS

By the way, are you coming over tonight?

CHRISTIAN
I might have to take a rain check.

SEBASTIAN
Oh, I see. It's come to that, has it? Very well. That's okay. That's okay.

HE LOOKS AWAY AND SOBS QUIETLY FOR A MOMENT

Look, I have to prepare. We shall talk anon.
CHRISTIAN
I don't speak any other languages.

WINSTON ENTERS WEARING THE SAME LADY BRACKNELL COSTUME.

SEBASTIAN
Assassin!

*MUSIC FROM "ONCE UPON A TIME IN THE WEST" CAN BE HEARD AS
WINSTON AND SEBASTIAN MOVE AROUND THE STAGE IN A MEXICAN
STAND-OFF.*

SEBASTIAN
Freddy, turn that fucking music off! *[MUSIC GOES OFF]* What are you doing?

WINSTON
Saving this turkey.

SEBASTIAN
We can't have two Lady Bracknells. You'll confuse the audience.

WINSTON
Nonsense. There you go. There's your style right there. We'll tell them it's some avant-garde Robert Le Page/arts festival bullshit.

CHRISTIAN RUNS OFF

SEBASTIAN
Where the hell is he going? Look, you can't play that fucking role. I am Lady Bracknell.

WINSTON
It needs a stronger actor. You're barely a director.

SEBASTIAN
Ah now the truth is out.

WINSTON
I love you to death. I don't want to see you fail. I'm only doing this for you.

SEBASTIAN
No, you're not. You're doing it for yourself!

WINSTON
You've always been jealous of me.

SEBASTIAN
Jealous of you? Oh puh-lease! Tell me what I have to be jealous of.

WINSTON
Well, for starters I had the breaks you *never* had.

SEBASTIAN
Breaks? What breaks would they be, pray tell?

WINSTON
When I was cast in Hedda Gabbler at college. I got the role of Lovborg. You got to be an usher. You hated me for it. Could never let it go.

SEBASTIAN
That was 25 years ago! You need to get a fucking support group.

WINSTON
I played it brill and you despised me for it.

SEBASTIAN
Despised you? Despised you? *[PAUSE]* Yes, I despised you! You were shrill and lifeless. I have an egg sandwich in my backpack that could have played Lovborg with more conviction.

WINSTON
See? Jealous! Oh and the fact that I can still get anyone I want sexually and you're on the way down. Begging blow jobs from pissed-as-newt straight guys too drunk to run. *"S'cuse me sir. Felch you for a fiver?"*

SEBASTIAN
And what about you? Don't see many offers coming your way. You're the fucking Vespa of sex.

WINSTON
What?

SEBASTIAN
Sure they look okay from a distance but nobody wants to be seen riding one!

CHRISTIAN RUNS ON IN THE SAME COSTUME AS THE OTHERS. THEY LOOK AT HIM.

WINSTON
I am beginning to think Shirley is an evil cunt.

SEBASTIAN
What are you wearing?

CHRISTIAN
Well, someone needs to be professional.

SEBASTIAN
Oh for Christ sakes. We cannot all play Lady Bracknell.

CHRISTIAN
Oh, is that who this is supposed to be?

SEBASTIAN
Maybe we should discuss this later?!!

WINSTON
Anyway, getting back to what we were talking about. I can get anyone I fancy.

SEBASTIAN
Really? Give me the name of something recent where no cash was exchanged for services rendered.

WINSTON
Well, I got him for starters.

SEBASTIAN
Oh, that stupid little cunt. Who cares?

CHRISTIAN
I'm not stupid.

SEBASTIAN AND WINSTON
Yes you are!

WINSTON
Even Stevie Wonder could see you're an idiot! Sort it out.

SEBASTIAN
[STARTS TO SOB] Well?

WINSTON
[RELENTING] Oh for fuck's sake. Come on chuckles.

HE STARTS TO DRAG CHRISTIAN OFF.

SEBASTIAN
Thank you. By the way we're cutting most of the show.

WINSTON
[STOPPING] What? When?

SEBASTIAN
Now. Tonight. We're doing it on the fly.

WINSTON
I don't even know what that means.

SEBASTIAN
Paraphrase you prick! Just try to keep the integrity of the piece.

WINSTON
What? Oh fuck me dead!

TINNY FANFARE.

SEBASTIAN
What is that?

CHRISTIAN
Start of the play I think. That'll be Freddy. He hates me.

SEBASTIAN
Who?

CHRISTIAN
Freddy. I dumped his arse.

SEBASTIAN
But we're not ready.

CHRISTIAN
Well, *I* bloody was. Let's see if he can get his *wife* to shove a dildo up him.

SEBASTIAN
But we have another *[LOOKING AT HIS WATCH]* ...oh shit. Places please, everyone!

WINSTON
[TO SEBASTIAN] By the way, the kid's off his tits. *[INDICATES CHRISTIAN]*

THEY EXIT.

SEBASTIAN
What??!! Mother-fuc…Okay, That's okay. You can get through this

SEBASTIAN MOVES THE TABLE DOWNSTAGE. HE STOPS AND STANDS FOR A MOMENT PUFFING AND CLUTCHING HIS CHEST.

Ooh that's not good. Jeezie creezy. Heart don't fail me now.

HE PICKS UP THE CHAIR. THERE IS A FART SOUND

Oops. Bowels, don't drop out of me now. *[YELLING INTO THE WINGS]* Okay Freddy, go!

BLACKOUT

SCENE FOUR

INTRO MUSIC. LIGHTS COME UP AGAIN. AFTER A PAUSE…

SEBASTIAN
[OFF] Hurry up, you fuckers!

WINSTON AND CHRISTIAN SCRAMBLE TO PLAY UPSTAGE TO AN IMAGINARY AUDIENCE.

CHRISTIAN *[AS JACK]*
When one is in town one amuses oneself. When one is in the country one amuses other people.

WINSTON *[AS ALGERNON]*
And who are the people you amuse?

CHRISTIAN *[AS JACK]*
Oh, neighbours, neighbours.

WINSTON *[AS ALGERNON]*
Got nice neighbours in your part of Shropshire?

CHRISTIAN *[AS JACK]*
Perfectly horrid! Never speak to one of them.

THEY LAUGH THEN MOVE THE FURNITURE BACK TO ITS ORIGINAL

POSITION WHILST TALKING.

WINSTON *[AS ALGERNON]*
How immensely you must amuse them! By the way, Shropshire is your county, is it not?

CHRISTIAN *[AS JACK]*
Don't even think about it.

WINSTON *[AS ALGERNON]*
Oh, ...er....um...by the way. I made up this imaginary friend called Bunbury. Any time I need to bugger off in a hurry I use him as an excuse. Very handy.

THEY CONTINUE TALKING ARM IN ARM AS THEY MOVE AROUND THE STAGE.

CHRISTIAN *[AS JACK]*
Lovely. I call myself Jack in the country and Earnest in town. Confuses the shit of everyone. That's handy as well. My ward Cecily lives in the country.

WINSTON *[AS ALGERNON]*
She sounds do-able.

THEY STOP.

CHRISTIAN *[AS JACK]*
Stay away from her. I am warning you. Now you need to sod off. My aunt Augusta, Lady Bracknell to you, is coming over. She hates your guts but she's bringing her hot daughter Gwendolen, who is quite up for it and *[SOUTHERN ACCENT]* I aims to make her mine.

WINSTON *[AS ALGERNON]*
Oh, and something about a cigarette case. Stop stealing my shit...blah, blah, blah.

WINSTON GOES TO EXIT BUT SEBASTIAN PUSHES HIM BACK ON WITH THE WALKING STICK AS LANE

WINSTON *[AS LANE]*
Lady Bracknell and her hot daughter Gwendolen.

HE RUNS OFF THEN SEBASTIAN AND WINSTON RUN BACK ON.

SEBASTIAN *[AS LADY BRACKNELL]*
Algernon, come show me some of the lovely tunes you've got planned for dinner.

WINSTON SPINS HIM AROUND IN A DOSEY DOE. SEBASTIAN IS CONFUSED BUT EXITS.

WINSTON *[AS GWENDOLEN]*
Yes, Mr. Worthing, what have you got to say to me?

CHRISTIAN *[AS JACK]*
You *know* what I have got to say to you.

WINSTON *[AS GWENDOLEN]*
Yes, but you don't say it.

CHRISTIAN *[AS JACK]*
Gwendolen, will you marry me?

WINSTON *[AS GWENDOLEN]*
Of course I will, darling. How long you have been about it!

CHRISTIAN *[AS JACK]*
My own one, I have never loved anyone in the world but you.

WINSTON *[AS GWENDOLEN]*
Yes, but men often propose for practice. I know my brother Gerald does.

WINSTON & CHRISTIAN
[BERKOFF STYLE] Cunt!

SEBASTIAN ENTERS.

SEBASTIAN *[AS LADY BRACKNELL]*
Mr. Worthing, get off your knees!

CHRISTIAN DROPS TO HIS KNEES THEN GETS UP AGAIN

WINSTON *[AS GWENDOLEN]*
Mamma, we are to be married.

SEBASTIAN *[AS LADY BRACKNELL]*
Bollocks! Your father and I will tell you when you are to be married and to

whom. Certainly not to this dick! Gwendolen, get out.

WINSTON EXITS. CHRISTIAN MOVES THE TABLE AND CHAIR AROUND TO THE BACK OF THE PLAYING AREA AND SEBASTIAN ADJUSTS HIS PLAYING TO THE FRONT AUDIENCE LOOKING A LITTLE CONFUSED.

Mr. Worthing, take a seat. *[TO CHRISTIAN UNDER HIS BREATH]* Don't speak. You're too slow. *[AS LADY BRACKNELL]* Mr. Worthing, a few questions. Do you smoke? Good. How old are you? 29? Good enough. Do you know everything or nothing? Pleased to hear it. Got any money? Investments are good. Land is useless. Politics? Tories, good. Everything else not good. Now to your parents… are they living? Both lost? To lose one parent, Mr. Worthing, may be regarded as a misfortune; to lose both looks like carelessness. What do you mean found? Found by whom? A Mr. Thomas Cardew perhaps? And where did this charitable gent find you?

HE WAITS FOR CHRISTIAN'S RESPONSE THEN ELBOWS HIM IN THE BALLS.

CHRISTIAN *[AS JACK]*
Oh, in a handbag.

SEBASTIAN *[AS LADY BRACKNELL]*
A handbag?

WINSTON YELLS THE LINE OFFSTAGE.

WINSTON
[OFFSTAGE] A handbag?

SEBASTIAN
[INTO THE WINGS] Fucker!

CHRISTIAN *[AS JACK]*
Yes. On the Brighton line.

SEBASTIAN *[AS LADY BRACKNELL]*
The line is immaterial. I would strongly advise you, Mr. Worthing, to try and acquire some relations as soon as possible.

CHRISTIAN *[AS JACK]*
I can produce the handbag at any moment. I really think that should satisfy you, Lady Bracknell.

SEBASTIAN *[AS LADY BRACKNELL]*
What has it to do with me? You can hardly imagine that I and Lord Bracknell would dream of allowing our only daughter to marry into a cloak-room and form an alliance with a parcel? Good morning, Mr. Worthing!

SEBASTIAN MOVES OFF SLOWLY THEN RUSHES TO EXIT AS WINSTON ENTERS

WINSTON *[AS ALGERNON]*
By the way, did you tell Gwendolen the truth about your being Ernest in town, and Jack in the country?

CHRISTIAN *[AS JACK]*
My dear fellow, the truth isn't quite the sort of thing one tells to a nice, sweet, refined girl. I'll say Ernest died in Paris of apoplexy.

WINSTON *[AS ALGERNON]*
But I thought you said that your ward Miss Cardew was a little too much interested in your poor brother Ernest? Have you told Gwendolen yet that you have an excessively pretty ward of just eighteen?

CHRISTIAN *[AS JACK]*
Cecily and Gwendolen are perfectly certain to be extremely great friends. I'll bet you anything you like that half an hour after they have met, they will be calling each other sister.

WINSTON *[AS ALGERNON]*
Women only do that when they have called each other a lot of other things first.

THEY LAUGH AS SEBASTIAN ENTERS AS MERRIMAN. CHRISTIAN CHANGES TO CECILY. WINSTON GOES TO EXIT BUT STOPS RIGHT IN FRONT OF SEBASTIAN. SEBASTIAN PUSHES HIM OFFSTAGE

SEBASTIAN *[AS MERRIMAN]*
Mr. Ernest Worthing has just driven over from the station. *[HE SHOVES WINSTON TO THE SIDE]* He has brought his luggage with him!

CHRISTIAN *[AS CECILY]*
Uncle Jack's brother? Did you tell him Mr. Worthing was in town?

SEBASTIAN *[AS MERRIMAN]*
Yes. He said he was anxious to speak to you privately for a moment.

CHRISTIAN *[AS CECILY]*
Ask Mr. Ernest Worthing to come here.

SEBASTIAN *[AS MERRIMAN]*
Yes, Miss. Hurrying all the way.

SEBASTIAN EXITS. WINSTON ENTERS AS ALGERNON.

WINSTON *[AS ALGERNON]*
You are my little cousin Cecily, I'm sure.

CHRISTIAN *[AS CECILY]*
You, I see from your card, are Uncle Jack's brother, my cousin Ernest, my *wicked* cousin Ernest.

WINSTON *[AS ALGERNON]*
You mustn't think that I am wicked.

CHRISTIAN *[AS CECILY]*
I hope you have not been leading a double life, pretending to be wicked and being really good all the time. That would be hypocrisy.

WINSTON *[AS ALGERNON]*
Cecily, ever since I first looked upon your wonderful and incomparable beauty, I have dared to love you wildly, passionately, devotedly, hopelessly. You will marry me, won't you?

CHRISTIAN *[AS CECILY]*
Of course, you silly fuck. *[HE SLAPS WINSTON HARD ACROSS THE FACE]* Why, in my mind we have been engaged for the last three months. I had heard so much about you I felt destined to be with you always. I broke it off for a little while but its back on now that you are here.

WINSTON *[AS ALGERNON]*
Lovely. *[HIS HAND GOES UP AND TWISTS CHRISTIAN'S NIPPLE, HARD]* Could you love me if my name wasn't Ernest?

CHRISTIAN *[AS CECILY]*
[CRINGING IN PAIN] Nope.

WINSTON *[AS ALGERNON]*
Glad we cleared that up.

SEBASTIAN ENTERS.

SEBASTIAN *[AS MERRIMAN]*
A Miss Fairfax has just called to see Mr. Worthing.

WINSTON
Shit!

WINSTON EXITS QUICKLY THEN COMES BACK ON.

SEBASTIAN *[AS MERRIMAN]*
On very important business…apparently.

SEBASTIAN EXITS. THEY SIT DOWN ON THE CHAIR AS CECILY AND GWENDOLEN. THEY RUSH THROUGH THE SCENE CUTTING EACH OTHER OFF AND GETTING ANGRY WITH EACH OTHER.

WINSTON *[AS GWENDOLEN]*
Your guardian?

CHRISTIAN *[AS CECILY]*
Yes, I am Mr. Worthing's ward.

WINSTON *[AS GWENDOLEN]*
Oh! It is strange he never mentioned to me that he had a ward. How secretive of him! If I may speak candidly…

CHRISTIAN *[AS CECILY]*
Pray do! I think that whenever one has anything unpleasant to say, one should always be quite candid.

WINSTON *[AS GWENDOLEN]*
Well, to speak with perfect candour, Cecily, I wish that you were fully for- ty-two, and more than usually plain for your age. Ernest has a strong upright nature.

CHRISTIAN *[AS CECILY]* I beg your pardon, Gwendolen, did you say Ern-est? It is not Mr. Ernest Worthing who is my guardian. It is his brother - his elder brother.

WINSTON *[AS GWENDOLEN]*
Ernest never mentioned to me that he had a brother.

CHRISTIAN *[AS CECILY]*
I am sorry to say they have not been on good terms for a long time.

WINSTON *[AS GWENDOLEN]*
Ah! That accounts for it. You are quite, quite sure that it is not Mr. Ernest Worthing who is your guardian?

CHRISTIAN *[AS CECILY]*
Quite sure. In fact, I am going to be his.

WINSTON *[AS GWENDOLEN]*
I beg your pardon. Mr. Ernest Worthing and I are engaged to be married.

CHRISTIAN *[AS CECILY]*
Bullshit! He is going to marry me.

WINSTON *[AS GWENDOLEN]*
Well we can soon sort this out. Here he comes now. Ernest! My own Ernest! Tell me you are not marrying this slapper?

CHRISTIAN RUNS IN A CIRCLE AND CHANGES TO JACK

CHRISTIAN *[AS JACK]*
To dear little Cecily? Of course not!

WINSTON *[AS GWENDOLEN]*
Thank you. You may kiss me. No tongue!

CHRISTIAN *[AS CECILY]*
I knew there must be some misunderstanding, Miss Fairfax. The gentle- man whose arm is at present round your waist is my guardian, Mr. John Worthing. Here is Ernest.

WINSTON *[AS GWENDOLEN]*
What? That's my cousin Algernon Moncrieff.

CHRISTIAN *[AS CECILY]*
Your name is not Ernest?

WINSTON *[AS ALGERNON]*
No. It's Algernon.

HE CHANGES QUICKLY.

WINSTON *[AS GWENDOLEN]*
Your name is not Ernest?

CHRISTIAN *[AS JACK]*
No. It's Jack

THEY LOOK AT EACH OTHER.

CHRISTIAN *[AS CECILY]*
Men are bastards!

WINSTON *[AS GWENDOLEN]*
Men are lying twats!

CHRISTIAN *[AS CECILY]*
Sister!

WINSTON *[AS GWENDOLEN]*
Sister!

THEY EMBRACE AND GIVE EACH OTHER A QUICK PECK ON THE CHEEK. THEY LOOK AT EACH OTHER THEN KISS AGAIN. THEY THEN KISS PASSIONATELY.

SEBASTIAN *[AS MERRIMAN]*
[OFF] Lady Bracknell.

SEBASTIAN ENTERS

[UNDER HIS BREATH TO WINSTON] Get off.

WINSTON EXITS BEWILDERED.

CHRISTIAN *[AS JACK]*
Lady Bracknell, your nephew is a scoundrel, a povvo and I suspect craves knob. What's worse he desires to marry my ward Cecily.

SEBASTIAN *[AS LADY BRACKNELL]*
I forbid it!

CHRISTIAN *[AS JACK]*
She is worth 180 thousand pounds.

SEBASTIAN *[AS LADY BRACKNELL]*
I fully approve. Just make sure she grows a chin and looks less dyke-ey.

CHRISTIAN *[AS JACK]*
And I will approve as long as I get to marry Gwendolen.

SEBASTIAN *[AS LADY BRACKNELL]*
No way Jose. You're background is suspect and you are related to a rail- way terminus.

CHRISTIAN *[AS JACK]*
The matter is entirely in your own hands. The moment you consent to my marriage with Gwendolen, I will most gladly allow your nephew to form an alliance with my ward.

SEBASTIAN *[AS LADY BRACKNELL]*
I shall think upon it.

SEBASTIAN MOVES SLOWLY THEN RUSHES OFF

SEBASTIAN *[AS MERRIMAN]*
[OFF] Dr. Chausable has arrived.

WINSTON RUNS BACK ON CONFUSED

WINSTON *[AS DR CHAUSABLE]*
Good morning to you. Where is Miss Prism? I want to marry her?

SEBASTIAN *[AS MERRIMAN]*
[OFF] But alas he cannot stay.

WINSTON *[AS DR CHAUSABLE]*
What?

SEBASTIAN
[OFF] Cut this bit! Get off!

WINSTON *[AS DR CHAUSABLE]*
Oh *[CLUTCHING HIS CHEST]* Oh...I think I'm dying. Of gout of the arse-flaps. I shan't be back.

HE EXITS AS SEBASTIAN ENTERS AGAIN LOOKING SLIGHTLY BEDRAGGLED, WIG ASKEW.

SEBASTIAN *[AS LADY BRACKNELL]*
Miss Prism! Did I bear you mention a Miss Prism? Is this Miss Prism a female of repellent aspect, remotely connected with education?

CHRISTIAN *[AS JACK]*
Miss Prism has been for the last three years Miss Cardew's esteemed governess. She is the most cultivated of ladies.

SEBASTIAN *[AS LADY BRACKNELL]*
It is obviously the same person. I must see her at once. Let her be sent for.

WINSTON COMES BACK ON AS MISS PRISM

SEBASTIAN *[AS LADY BRACKNELL]*
Prism! Twenty-eight years ago, Prism, you left Lord Bracknell's house, Number 104, Upper Grosvenor Street, in charge of a perambulator that contained a baby of the male sex. You never returned. Prism! Where is that baby?

WINSTON *[AS MISS PRISM]*
[BAD SCOTTISH ACCENT, THE OTHER LOOKS HORRIFIED] Lady Bracknell, I admit with shame that I do not know. On the morning of the day you mention I prepared as usual to take the baby out in its perambulator. I had also with me a somewhat old, but capacious hand-bag in which I had intended to place the manuscript of a work of fiction that I had written. *[SNEARING AT SEBASTIAN]* Cum Guzzlers Under The Loggia. In a moment of mental abstraction, I deposited the manuscript in the bassinette and the baby in the *[BIG HAMMY SCOTTISH ACCENT]* hand- bag.

CHRISTIAN *[AS JACK]*
But where did you deposit the hand-bag?

WINSTON *[AS MISS PRISM]*
Do not ask me, Mr. Worthing.

CHRISTIAN *[AS JACK]*
I insist on knowing where you deposited the *[BIG HAMMY SCOTTISH ACCENT]* 'hand-bag' that contained that infant.

WINSTON *[AS MISS PRISM]*
I left it in the cloak-room of one of the larger railway stations in London. Victoria. The Brighton line.

CHRISTIAN *[AS JACK]*
Is this the handbag?

HE LOOKS AROUND THEN GRABS THE DUCK OFF THE TABLE AND PRETENDS TO BE HOLDING A HANDBAG.

WINSTON *[AS MISS PRISM]*
[GRABBING THE DUCK OFF HIM] Oh! The bag is undoubtedly mine. I am de- lighted to have it so unexpectedly restored to me.

CHRISTIAN *[AS JACK]*
Miss Prism, more is restored to you than this hand-bag. I was the baby you placed in it. Mother, I forgive you.

HE TRIES TO EMBRACE HER]

WINSTON *[AS MISS PRISM]*
Mr. Worthing! I am unmarried! There is the lady who can tell you who you really are. Oh, there is good Dr. Chausable in the garden with a gun.

SOUND OF GUNSHOT. WINSTON FLINGS THE DUCK IN THE AIR. CHRISTIAN CATCHES IT AND PUTS IT BACK ON THE TABLE.

Oh, I have been shot. I shall retire.

WINSTON RUNS OFF LEAVING THE OTHERS SLIGHTLY BEWILDERED

CHRISTIAN *[AS JACK]*
Er...ah...Lady Bracknell, I hate to seem inquisitive, but would you kindly inform me who I am?

SEBASTIAN *[AS LADY BRACKNELL]*
You are the son of my poor sister, Mrs. Moncrieff, and consequently Algernon's elder brother.

CHRISTIAN *[AS JACK]*
Algy's elder brother! Then I have a brother after all. At the time when Miss Prism left me in the hand-bag, had I been christened already?

SEBASTIAN *[AS LADY BRACKNELL]*
Every luxury that money could buy, including christening, had been lavished on you by your fond and doting parents.

CHRISTIAN *[AS JACK]*
Then I was christened! That is settled. Now, what name was I given? Let me know the worst.

SEBASTIAN *[AS LADY BRACKNELL]*
Being the eldest son you were naturally christened after your father.

CHRISTIAN *[AS JACK]*
Yes, but what was my father's Christian name?

WINSTON RUNS BACK ON DRESSED AS LADY BRACKNELL AGAIN AND ECHOES SEBASTIAN'S LINES. SEBASTIAN IS FURIOUS AND MOVES CLOSER TO HIM.

SEBASTIAN & WINSTON *[AS LADY BRACKNELL]*
I cannot at the present moment recall what the General's Christian name was. But I have no doubt he had one and it would appear in any military directory of that period.

CHRISTIAN *[AS JACK]*
Ah. The Army Lists of the last forty years are here. *[HE LOOKS AROUND, REALISES THERE IS NO BOOK THEN PRETENDS TO OPEN A BOOK AND LOOK THROUGH IT]* Markby, Migsby, Mobbs, Moncrieff! Lieutenant 1840, Captain, Lieutenant-Colonel, Colonel, General 1869, Christian names, Ernest John. I always told you, *[GLARING AT WINSTON]* Gwendolen, my name was Ernest, didn't I? Well, it *is* Ernest after all. I mean it naturally *is* Ernest.

SEBASTIAN & WINSTON *[AS LADY BRACKNELL]*
Yes, I remember now that the General was called Ernest, I knew I had some particular reason for disliking the name.

CHRISTIAN *[AS JACK]*
It is a terrible thing for a man to find out suddenly that all his life he has been speaking nothing but the truth.

SEBASTIAN & WINSTON *[AS LADY BRACKNELL]*
My nephew, you seem to be displaying signs of triviality.

CHRISTIAN *[AS JACK]*
On the contrary, Aunt Augusta...sss, I've now realised for the first time in my life the vital Importance of Being Earnest.

THEY ALL LAUGH. A MOBILE PHONE STARTS RINGING. SEBASTIAN

CASUALLY WALKS UP TO THE TABLE, PICKS UP THE DUCK AND COMES DOWNSTAGE. WINSTON CURTSEYS. AS HE COMES UP SEBASTIAN SLAMS HIM ACROSS THE HEAD WITH THE DUCK.

BLACKOUT

End